DALE JACOBSON

A WALK BY THE RIVER

A LONG POEM

MINNESOTA

RED DRAGONFLY PRESS

2004

Original wood engravings by Gaylord Schanilec.

Typefaces are Californian & Berkeley, both
digital adaptations of Goudy's California Old Style.

ISBNs:
1-890193-38-0 (deluxe letterpress edition—30 copies)
1-890193-39-9 (regular letterpress edition—70 copies)
1-890193-40-2 (print-on-demand trade edition)

Printed in cooperation with the Southeastern
Minnesota Arts Council, Inc. through funding from the
Minnesota State Legislature.

Print-on-demand trade edition
printed by BookMobile in St.Paul, Minnesota.

Published by: Red Dragonfly Press
press-in-residence
Anderson Center
P. O. Box 406
Red Wing, MN 55044

A WALK BY THE RIVER

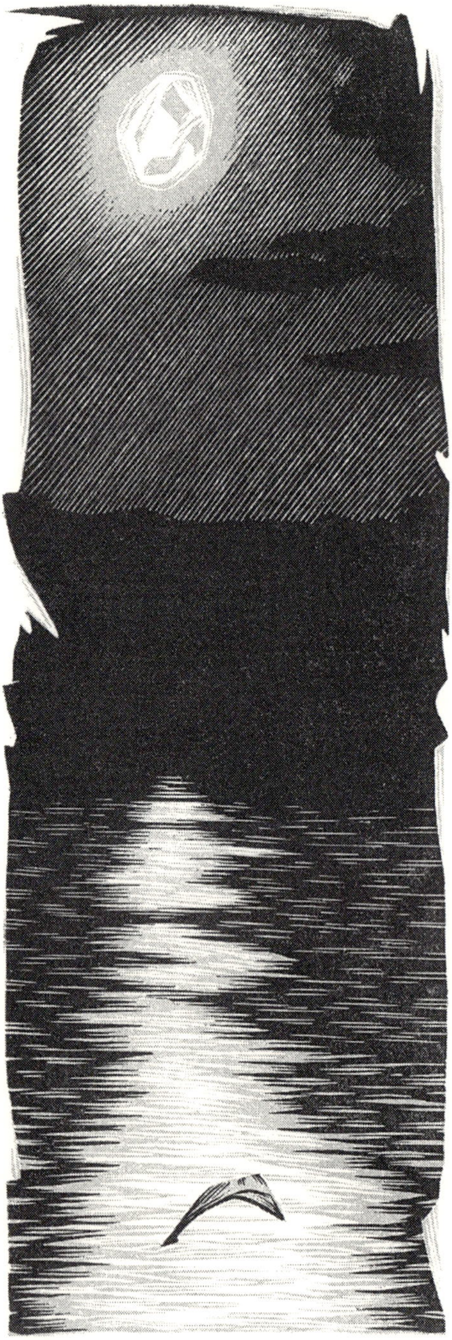

If this river were another time,
if I were walking home
like a child in the night,
what could I remember?

PART ONE

I.

I went for a walk by the river,
summoned by a drift or turn in the air,
unsure I didn't hear a flock
of ghostly birds disturb the trees.
Or perhaps it was the hollow whirls of water,
vortexes turning on emptiness,
that called me. Years ago it seemed
my name had been lost—swept away
by wind to a place where an ancient
turtle had dropped its head to earth.

This was a season of drought.
The river was shallow.
This was a season when
even the cockleburs looked shriveled,
those thorny orbs the size of eyes,
their dark centers sending out
blind hooks in all directions.

Along the burdock-burdened shore
the earth was cracked like terra cotta.
It was a spring when the earth
was secretive as a dead prophet.
Tree roots sent out long thin threads
seeking moisture. Far beneath
were the fossils the eons had stored.

Far beyond and hidden by the arid
afternoon sky the galaxies turned.
The shallow river flowed between
the archives of ossified tombs
and the fierce whorls of plasma,
between the physics of stone and fire,
which continued to obey laws
older than the river, the enormous
span of their remote seasons . . .

II.

This river which ran through
a decade of my life in Fargo,
another decade in Grand Forks,
this Red River, this road for water
has reflected and lost
countless images of swooping birds,
the moon has cast its cold
columns of light upon its surface,
river flowing north the Norsemen
navigated south, these waters
capture from the air
invisible motes of dust.

And before the dust goes down,
finally loses itself to saturation,
it warns: there is also a road of dust,

there is also a cycle of dust,
the tribe of dust does not have kings
but lasts longer than empires,
the tribe of dust builds cities
in the corners of ceilings in abandoned
rooms, in condemned houses—
where water no longer visits.

III.

A crow flew up startled—caw! caw! caw!—
an annoyed black rag, a flapping
indignity. A flock of sparrows,
an elastic congregation reshaping itself,
rose up in the distance, converged
in the nearest elm tree, their notes
a nervous chatter, a riot of discord
interrupted by mysterious pauses.

The sky was a wide and bright
translucence—a passive blue
ascending into its own abstraction.
It was so intensely the same I imagined
something unnatural wanted to happen,
out of its expanse a blaze would ignite
a crackling red flash, an electric net
inventing itself into the horizons!

It was like a desert sky—beneath which,
in the shallow river, something leapt.

IV.

The color of extinction
is the color of a shark
made from pale moonlight
diving in the wheat field
at the edge of the dusk.

Extinction is the hollow dark
that no one can pronounce
in the mouth of the skull—
a word so still even the dead
in the buried empires of Sumer
have not been dead
long enough to speak it.

It is the drop of water
whose absence meant
worlds were not born.
Extinction is so efficient
even the mote of dust
balanced on the claw
of the dead cat
floats above it.

V.

History is the story of ruined peoples.

The river goes on flowing
indecently oblivious, opening
deep doors of its own darkness.

There the shadows of sons
flow into the shadows of fathers
which flow into the shadows
of their fathers—a long regression
of sons, songs, daughters,
mothers and fathers in the murky
night of water toward the deep
undersea currents...

Water,
which unlike stone,
denies itself a history
and refuses monuments,
says everything seeks
the level of water, seeks
the level of ocean
where the waves fall out
of themselves, bury themselves
like forgetting...

VI.

I saw the eagle swoop down
and lift the fish into sky!
The fish lolling too near
the light, a heavy shadow
seen by the gliding bird,
the hunting eye hunger-driven,
seeking survival by chance...

Any fish would feed the bird,
but *this* fish, this *one*, thrashing
and wobbling, was lifted
to the altitude of departure,
its own hunger became
the sky's emptiness as the river
closed upon its absence.

River and wind continued
in their currents,
water and dust indifferent
if bird starved
or fish swam free.

Both bird and fish
in time would die,
in time both lose time.

Did the fish shed
the weight of its pain,
in the wake of its death
a long loss
weaving through the breeze,
something infinite released—
or did its broken moment
fall
like a drop of water
from its fin
back into the river,
which went on darkly flowing?

The bird-fish creature
flapped beyond the trees,
one half alive, one half dead
(life consuming death—
death sleeping inside life),
while wind and river
both swept on—returning
from nowhere—nor departing...

VII.

With the complacent resurrection of the swift skies,
within the calm of a yawn at early light
reside dangers

in dust that finds
the tip of the tongue.

No one can predict what will incite the dust—
a passing butterfly or breeze—no one knows
the probabilities of the air, its endless
swirls, the multitudes of dust armed
with morbid viruses, those invisible keys
that unlock the distances to whose death?

I rose this morning late as I like,
decided to walk this river,
knowing it is possible to drown
in a quarter inch of water.

I rose with certitude, a conviction
the day would hold me—but
shadows on the water
somehow remind me there exist
black holes beyond these skies
capable of crushing to a pin's head
two billion stars, as if Shiva,
mechanistic monster of the cosmic dance,
blinked.

There are infinite ways for the infinite
quiet power
to annihilate
one life.

What don't I know that I mourn
each life like some grieving doctor
whose hands are heavy wings
as the hospital goes on dying?

To whom or what should I confess,
as if it were a crime to mention
like Trakl: *I'm tired of the immense slaughter*?

Last winter at my cabin
I found a chipmunk
that had taken a wrong turn,
somehow upset a piece of wood
and launched from the woodpile
a bucket that must have landed
perfectly over its panicked body,
imprisoning it above the frost-hardened ground.
And there that night it froze,
curled up on itself, the lightning
on its back caught. It looked asleep
except that its eyes were shut
too tight, as if protecting its life.

No one in a millennium could predict
such an event. When Carthage was built,
no one could imagine the Romans
would burn it to the ground,
not the Romans themselves. No one
thought Pompeii would end entombed

in stone ash fallen from the sky.
Ash and dust, these cities.

Those long-dead citizens the earth
took back into itself—do they listen
in some strange twilight for
the slightest tilt of a lead-grey moon
balanced on a glass thread,
the moment the universe shifts
and time begins again?

It is gone, whatever it was is gone—
whatever its shape, it learns loss—
the next morning continues toward
the next evening where the stars
might be clear—but there is no
direction left for the dead thing.

VIII.

There is no ceremony for dead animals.
Their bone and decaying sinew, the energy
of those things, uninhabited bodies,
goes into earth and sky. What remains
is their ragged wreckage along the trails,
signs no one can read or follow.

Here the emperor's mandate is without
meaning: *fiat justitia, ruat caelum.*

He who had a moment of power
imposed no justice and then learned
where all empires end. For animals,
who are innocent, the law simply says:
this is the moment and place of death
and all the world in nature comes to loss.
Beyond those skulls and teeth,
the limits of wind and dust,
no republics pass laws against the poor,
no tyrannies whisper secrets...

The river is Eros, the river is life. This
trail is worn by the bicycles of children.
Exuberance takes them, the world flourishes.
Yesterday, a child was swallowed
in a gravel pit sinkhole
as the conveyer belt removed sand
beneath him. The fine silica,
catching the sun as it shifted,
closed over, obeyed gravity—
took him out of the light.
Sand and circumstance were fatal caprice,
the intersection of mass and emptiness
that could not distinguish a child's life,
a mineral cascade collapsing through
all his future years...

Where do the dead animals go?
Do their eyes burn darkly in the death

of stars, in black holes beyond our events,
in curves our horizons can never encompass,
where they invite the children,
ageless in each of us, from life?

Teeth and cold
never feel
the pain they give.
Water does not know
the drowning terror.
fire is fury
that consumes its fuel
with indifferent heat.
Sand seeks silence
closing the mouth
of a young boy,
knows nothing of
mute panic.

What can a finite body know of the infinite forces
that collapse galaxies? Where do the animals go?

If we ignore Heraclitus and stroll
only as far as the shadows fall
at the edge of town, then the twilight
seems serene, without conflict, the fierce
winds far away. Some insist all is ordered,
assume God knows what God does,
is awake, or gives a damn.

But the evidence is not so easy.
When the fierce winds descend, whirl
and tear and lightnings course
swift currents without map and trees
rear in the depth of night and crash,
something irrational rules whose freedom
storms far beyond the intervals of my watch.

In a universe so immense each second
a supernova explodes, what address
can I give my house? Though my fingertips
touch all distances, what does distance teach?

I went to Ireland once, Celtic mystical country
under Catholic skies, island the ocean gnaws.
There I saw cathedrals fallen into the ground.
In Cashell I saw the stone walls open to wind and stars,
an empty shell, a nave for the nuances of rain,
its priests long ago murdered by Cromwell,
who knew another God from another country.
In my time the American God, no less righteous
than any other, still leaves workers dead or poor
from the great wars. Neither nature nor God
has lately spoken justice, and I can't read the birds.

I know the stone angels of cathedrals
can neither survive cannon fire, nor
stand on the ocean. I know all rivers
come at last to the sea, where sharks,

with eyes more keen than those of prophets
in a world whose ways are water, were born
350 million years ago—
and have been eating ever since.

IX.

I see water turn on either side
of a small island, I hear the slight
song of water lapping against
shore and against water,
I smell the long and wide day
filled with pollen and scent of earth,
I feel the breeze.

Earth,
this bright island turning in space,
will change color—its forests
will at last flash, consumed
by no second flood but by
the engulfing fires, the expanding
nova of the self-extinguishing sun—

fierce dying light
will then dim and fail
inward—
'And kingdoms naked—
O Thou Hand of fire'

—crushing itself
into a white fist,
a cooling core of carbon.

I think how the river, when
it erodes this small island,
will continue on with its dark
currents toward the powerful sea.

Where will have gone the energy of sharks,
those swift ancient hunters flung
into the currents of space after the earth
is brightly snapped out of time?

If time can collapse—and space—
if the river, like the ancient serpent
in mythologies, devours itself,
what is the condensed period
at the end of all the varied songs
and fires and their winds—the silent
seed at the end of our sun
into which the ellipses of time
fall, the distances fold themselves?

X.

We find ourselves in a bewildering world
—Stephen W. Hawking

The universe seemed then,
when I was a child in the great house,
stranger than a wizard's trick,
myself a newcomer (somehow)
to the old ways of thunder and dust,
the night a dark river without shore,
endless expanse of swirling galaxies,
and my own hand a mystery of touch...

We name this river the Red,
who live by it, who need it,
but always the river loses itself,
elegiac waters, perpetual falling...

My home town can never return,
gone with those childhood voices
that once sang and fell far into dusk.

I felt then among the dark trees,
in those young years,
their presence just beyond
the huge sound of my footsteps,
in the twilight: our ancestors,
in the wind, in the voice of the river,

in those mysterious valleys—
distances,
                origins,
                        remote hours
I somehow knew...

What *is* the story of the universe,
older than the hills—a blind eye
that decided to dream, an intense
patience that invented time?
Or is the universe a lost expanding hand
learning the void within itself,
touching only the void beyond?

I've made inquiries—but always
the process of things veils the purpose.

From within the vault of this skull,
with its faulty eyes that require correction,
within the solitude of this body
whose arrangements with time are more
personally expensive than I would like,
always living toward its private catastrophe
which the river will not notice,
this body whose limits of intelligence
I was given, whose personal name
has less permanence than a dead turtle's roof
—with these senses that cannot sense
their own end, nor know knowing ended

and will cease to know their own past,
what can I, *whosoever I am*, know?

Does dust vibrate silently with ancient news?
Is the wilderness of stars ecstatic dance of fire?
Will the rivers locked in my eyes
release a darkness into darkness?

River,
          stone,
                    wind—
                              these shifting foundations
that fall—if grief is the power that puzzles me,
dark companion, its ancestor is gravity.

Home and its loss is gravity.
Gravity is the river that erodes stone.
Gravity is the journey and its station,
the locomotive diminishing, the bird
falling into the horizon though the horizon
remains the same—gravity is the bridge
spanning its own time—it is the ocean
where the rivers of the mountains kneel,
gravity brings the winds low,
it is the sleeping ear that mutes all words,
the keeper of the massive planets and stars,
gravity the encompassing zero
great as the expanses of light-years,
the million million galaxies cast across

the vast night whose sum of infinity is
nothing...

Gravity is the center of all my griefs,
lover I don't know who attracts me.

XI.

The physical evidences are remains
locked in rock, lineages that rose and died,
skeletons like hieroglyphs elaborating a mystery.

What can I decipher from the scraps and pieces
the most curious of my kind have gathered,
uncertain I know the right questions?

When Charles Darwin translated Adam Smith
into the economics of biology,
and Herbert Spencer made the individual
supreme, each one fit to survive,
then William Paley's great watchmaker
ran out of time—and the intellectuals of the age
drove a stake through the heart of Karl Marx,
but applauded Carl Jung, who though
he saw a system greater than one, made
the collective unconscious personal myth.

All these names in great debate!—
but a penny tossed into the river is lost

whether thoughts be right or wrong,
and the long system of the river joins
the cycles of the sea—and the moon is serene.

Should I celebrate my ancestor, first
vertebrate, the fish *Cephalaspis*, who swam
pushing its bony mask it wore for a face,
whose name means "head shield"?

Dear Grandmother-father Shield,
I speak of you who did not speak,
who plowed your way through days
jawless and imprisoned within
your own armor, your mask become
your legend, who are now extinct...

Though you did not dream
in comedy, murder or soul,
from your obscure need we somehow
came, who take into war *our* shields,
who are organized into classes
against ourselves, wear masks harder
than yours against the poor—and construct
intellectual helmets against pity...

All seems dependent upon these bodies
we give to each other or kill.
Born from the dark silent currents,
from a secret genetic symmetry

that embraced itself like a ladder,
out of the sea these bodies we inhabit
arrived as though they could stand—
in the lucid clarity of light:
and speak—
                    though speech was like
hunger need fire rage grief:
and endure—
                    though endurance was more
than surviving climates, but the fierce
rose burning in its deep cool core.

Dear Grandmother-father Shield,
silence swimming the rivers, did one eye
glimpse terror while the other forgot it?
In the dark waters where change is endless
but also blind, how did your wandering
hunger walk out of water onto land,
invent a road, take flight—
eyes born of water follow their vision
into the original vast night of swirling
fires—and from the arid moon astronauts
gaze down upon the earth's oceans?

From your primal silence we voyage into ours,
that deep mirror measured in light years,
face of the undeciphered universe, stars
so distant their light has yet to arrive,
while the poor, whose faces we cannot see,
are cloaked in a darkness no stars penetrate.

Out of our history constructed upon
the shadow of one dictator propped against
the shadow of another, leaving nothing
substantial for the poor, suppose we invent
something like another *kind* of water, a language
that washes over us (after so much loose fire!)
—and washes away all this long memory of war,
from a savage baptism an elemental communion.

Say, for the sake of saying, my tribe
saves itself, as yours did not, say the light
becomes at last an invention beyond itself,
a way of seeing each face is our own—and hunger—
light moving at the speed of recognition—
say we learn these things as if a destiny
actually spoke through the eternal silences,
those great extinctions: Grandmother-father Shield,
how could that news awaken your fossil stare
stamped in rock, all that time of evolution
return to your eyes turned to stone?

Where have they gone, those remote relatives
with different styles from hair to scales,
lives devoured, all those other kinds not kin,
species that came and went, each death separate?

What crystal eye pulls together the parts,
from the long past, which has suffered—
all these varied creatures, all unlike ourselves

who like ourselves share earth and die:
who are *they*?—animals and insects who
like ourselves know nothing of not continuing—
those 'sea creatures left stranded on dry sand'
Pliny the Younger noticed as the waters
were sucked away just before Mount Vesuvius
buried Pompeii and Herculaneum in fire?

Species go extinct like weather changes,
sea changes, everything but the underlying silence...

It is with these questions that logic falters,
becomes useless as a feather in the water,
a fish on stone under the cold moon...

I've killed many squirrels and rabbits when
I once hunted, saw their bodies surrendered,
become something unfamiliar to the life
that had made them quick, the mechanism broken.

These apparent separate selves that lose
themselves and leave no apparition,
no proof of who they were beyond habits
of lost uses—bodies drained of energy once
coherent—skeletons impressed in stone—
the evidence suggests they are no more
than events that came, acted, and ceased,
the hunger that drove them finally emptied
of itself—each fish, turtle, horse, bird—each person—

once finished, devoured by the great infinities,
the galaxies that dome the dark hills.

There is no difference between one dead thing
and another, and only time between
the living and the dead, the shadows of the day.
Entropy dislocates all locations: my home town
is long gone and Epicurus is finally defeated
by the physical fates—all atoms become equal and one.

Where does our absence take us?

I could say we are disguises of what we ourselves
don't know we mask, the differences between
species and species, and brother and brother
only flames of one fire—or say raindrops
returning to one river, fire and water
themselves masks of the Original Silence,
'source of the longest river'—the stillness
virtually wavering and not wavering
'between two waves of the sea'...

But the fact is: the senses can make no sense
of their annihilation—and so we sensibly fear
we are masks of a cruel dilemma:

Grandmother-father Shield whose shield
did not save, fish whose bones have become
stone, who swam into the mineral archives,

we fear the permanence of your departure—
and ours, these disposable bodies, our faces
like yours masks that fall away, days the rains
and rivers reclaim, leaving nothing but
the *nothingness* of the universe hiding from
*it*self, like dust falling in a falling wind,
a thin sound sounding only fury or fear...

XII.

The river knows no questions, swirls
past the tree tilting from the shore—
one branch sunk into the water
sheds the long hair of weaving turbulence
as if giving up the last signatures of itself.
Eddies whip away into a roiling galaxy
of whirlpools, liquid light spinning toward
dark centers like inverse stars, small
momentary vortexes that dissolve dust
and themselves dissolve into the river,
their hollow identities at last drowned,
like the souls of a dying tree, though
the sky remains vast and the skin of water,
the shuffling roof of the river, goes on
building and tearing apart its own
six-sided lattice of atoms, the river whose logic
is change perpetually reconstructing itself,
though always the same journey toward salt,
the wide modulating currents of the sea...

The river knows no name, flows on
without knowing the difference between
now and that rumored moment Christ
came to do strange things with water,
nor five centuries earlier when Thales
of Miletus, first philosopher, named water
'the one essential element'—the river
continues out of its older origins,
without a nation, without appointments,
without heaven or concern for light or dark,
water whose only horizon is itself,
the endless and curved waters of the sea.

It does not matter how much time
we give to the river, which moves its sand
downstream one hundred miles
in a million years—does not matter
how long we follow its journey, we end
at the ocean, wall of water that curves
into itself, and beneath are buried
our great ships, the bones of our thoughts,
those hulls of our days that once dazzled,
irrelevant to water as our questions,
our reason, science, our explorations,
our lasting longing for its secrets...

Water reveals no image other than
our own reflection lost in its depth—
or the image of wind the dust rides,
our absence, the color of the sky...

PART TWO

In any case, it is too difficult for me,
and I wish I had been a movie
comedian or something of the sort
and had never heard of physics.
—Wolfgang Pauli

My theology is a simple muddle.
I cannot look at the universe as the result
of blind chance, yet I see no evidence
of beneficent design in the details.
—Charles Darwin

I.

The hawk floats above the clearing,
working the wind—hunting any small
motion inside the circle of its hunger.

Did birds, whose habits of height we admire,
enter the sky by no design—those wings
whose turnings our superstition once read
as signatures of future events,
evolve from fans to flight by random fortune,
wings lift to wind as caprice upon caprice?

If wings, those sky-collecting arms, took to air
by chance, what is our voice—song born from soil,
flight of vowels heavy with earth's consonants?
The logic of the question terrifies Christians
more than hell and no star-shouldering general
dares ask: *whether indifferent chaos builds infinity.*

Where do we belong within anonymous night
darkening equally over a dictionary and a stone?
Are these words that name and claim a world
more than odd callings to the weather?

I think back upon the struggle of my ancestors,
my species, those who followed the rivers,

who began to say before Aristotle the useful
roots and leaves and learn the habits of animals...

Could spear, that deadly verb, have remained
unchiseled and tongue dumb as mud, could
poetry remain unsung in the wild terrains
where creatures honed their cries on moonlight
with no myth to sail to the far shores of the stars?

In a world where all tongues at last turn
to windy dust, what does it matter that somehow
someone far back learned to speak so someone
now can say the word 'entropy' or 'loss'?

And when the body comes to the place where
the body can go no further—and the cells
finally give up and fall away from each other
and break apart, *whose experience is that*?

What happens to the long meditation
the cells had unified to create when,
as if learning an insouciance within,
they surrender at last to everything beyond?

II.

These bodies we are arrived—
from secret resonances and rhymes,

atoms humming a quadrillion
vibrations per second, arrived
through the windings and weavings
of chromosomal time, far origins—
sun-glint on water and alchemy
of water transforming itself...

And from within came the voice:
and what was learned was told—
water descending, the wind
rising and falling in the trees,
the cool stillness of dusk
where the ghosts of memory
ride the light down like another life,
a world always separating...

Though silence was deeper than sleep
and older than the first dawn,
the voice that could call nothing back
spoke as though each day depended
upon its word: each mote of dust,
the dew and the opening blossoms,
river that quarreled with stone,
the winds that often sounded like the sea,
cry of the hunting hawk,
the shadow that mocked the sun
and night that consumed the shadow,
gravity and its attendant grief—
the voice spoke as though fame mattered.

In a world where fame is a white crest
riding the ocean wave falling out of itself,
voice spoke the distance between
the tides, the time to the new moon
and the starved owl, and yet spoke
as though speaking were something
necessary in a world always departing,
though names came to mean absences,
and vowels held a hollow sound haunting
evening, the sound of a flute speaking
the color of bone inside the color of dusk,
the voice spoke like a soul of origins:
ancient, full and present,
in the center of everything,
in the center of coming and going
and winds that erased alphabets,
these bodies we are came and spoke
as though they could abide.

III.

They say memory was born from
the sense of smell, from the 'dark cloak'
of the primitive brain, a sniff to shape
the odors of danger, the stalking terrors
that moved in the night—a way of survival.

And with its inward world came dreaming,

the psychic hunt...
                    longing for the location
of the serene secret, the glint of the raindrop
like a lucent seed...
                    free-falling meditation...
the source...
              distance without danger...

Neanderthals buried their dead in a bed of flowers—
a safe haven at last—in the lastness sweet-smelling
fading of memory an act of tenderness,
the best that could be done—

Yesterday and the year before are places
on another planet spun away and drowned
in our eyes when we look into the river
and think it is something else, and see
worlds we know within ourselves—
dim and distant noons fixed by their passions—
midnight plateaus where we thought legends lasted,
the words our parents and grandparents spoke,
whose hands are the winds that have become
our losses...

In those places and hours we remember,
they are always the same, those people
who no longer answer their names
and repeat struggles that once meant the world.
They belong to a solitude not their own,

players of a drama seen by an audience of one,
yourself, learning and relearning
and trying to see clearly, trying to feel clearly
before the curtain, a fatal darkness, falls—
and all loss collapses inward upon the keeper.

Those ghosts of ourselves guide us to where
we can no longer arrive, phantom fires and furies
continually consuming the nostalgic sky—and yet:
that aureate world that once seemed home
haunts—like the orange light that filters down
just after a storm clears, eerie and familiar—
when all is locked in an ionized atmosphere
that seems new and ancient at once:

something like origin, the road the old dawn
walks with the eyes of a child, remote hour
the passions seek when they fix the past
in their long light—calling a place they know
and are known in a world they haven't learned
to relinquish: everything shifting from that far
prime nuclear flurry of a sun-dancing hive.

IV.

All seems decided by survival.
But if survival is the equation of one
added to nothing, it cannot balance itself

over the abyss of nothing—means
nothing
if nothing goes beyond.

If I reduce things to their mechanics,
the world becomes the taste of ash
when ditches are burned in spring,
or the dull pain of working a poor tooth:
all our tools are tragic implements—
and memory, feeling, imagination
tell us too much, suggest too much.
What remains is survival—and after,
a fly buzzing in an empty skull.

The river survives. History seems to survive,
the few
gain land,
plan power,
survive
(while the poor remain anonymous).

They become dust under the cold light of stars,
the generations—those ancestors whose deaths
became our road: history is our collective memory,
though owned by those that own the nations.

If we remember too much, those images
cannot recast their light and shadows,
they don't reconstruct demolished walls

or create loaves of bread from air,
help metabolism, bring rain, or pay rent—
shapes and shades from the past remain
without power though power seems to decide
if this village lives or that bird sings,
an ant hill swirls into a tornado's attic,
or a city climbs a column of fire.

If we feel more than is required to breathe,
perhaps that surplus is evidence:
when the river's passing pulls us
and we feel gravity in our lives,
feel our own passing and passage through
the long griefs and the mind pauses—
studies a shimmering dream fire
upon the waters, light beyond ourselves,
connected—light burning within
ourselves and far away on the hills
like thin deer walking the horizons...

If we imagine another kind of world
where power does *not* govern,
perhaps power and survival are
the poorer tools,
                    tools the poor need—
but have fought all this history long
to invent a world beyond,
just past a stone's throw, a cruise missile—
a world imagined almost as if remembered

when, like a child falling into wonder,
we gaze upon light upon the water...

V.

And what if the ghost of that fish
came swimming up the river,
a dark slow ripple out of the past,
Cephalaspis, first vertebrate now extinct?

Ugly old agnathous head-hulk of a fish
who with no Ph.D. but a backbone,
changed everything: your descendants
climbed onto land, learned or invented
other instructions, shifted their shapes,
traveled and transformed terra firma.

Grandmother-father Head-hulk,
what became of you?
Does your backbone
in its fossil home vibrate a stone music,
an echo of your life, resonances that swim
the matrix of the universe, weaving
harmonious waves across light years?

I think further back to primordial origins,
when mom and dad equaled narcissism,
the first cell for an instant forming the sign
of infinity before dividing to create itself,

omnis cellula e cellula, committees of cells
creating policies, building life and—
larger hungers, great lizards
that devoured several million years,
but the largest hunger still starving—
not *Eros*, but *agape*, whose food is feeling.

I cannot say where you went, or what
you were—or are—or have become,
Grandmother-father Head-hulk, ancient life,
if you swim the universe through cosmic rivers,
or perhaps swim through us who are
a moment in the river of time, if time exists—
I do not know what became of those far cousins
Australopithecus africanus, boisei, robustus,
Homo habilis, Homo erectus, or what will
become of (named by the sapience of Linnaeus)
Homo sapiens sapiens myself—or that other
species, Homo Ph.D. elite intellectualis,
names in the ancient house of Latin:
Pallida Mors aequo pulsat pede
pauperum tabernas regumque turris.

The trees are neither open nor closed
where our ancestors took refuge,
those branches a place for children or
the rope that hangs the man who swings
while leaves
flutter.
            The shadow of the nineteenth century,

like a dead dry branch, still touches
the land. And even though water wears
no mask the river remains inscrutable,
sometimes tossing a blaze of light like a sword.

But I know all is connected, I am transitory life
in a home that transcends me, the river
a continuity that will continue after
these days drop like visions into my dark.

All born from the same fires, those supernovae
that gave birth to planets, if beauty exists
beyond terror or despair, if beatitude exists
in the cinders of stars, the dark ciphers,
it is not defeated by the mean habits of my
dying country, whose meager imagination
ruins the poor—and leaves boredom
the player of solitaire with cards of wind.

In a universe of mysterious method,
fibonacci series or Planck's Constant, and
unpredictable fierce storms, chaos within order,
a universe of universal change—yet:
Grandmother-father Head-hulk,
my small moment is connected to yours—
across space and time joined—
and though your ugly face seems hardly worth
being cast in rock, we who invented the poor
are hardly worth asking about beauty.

The river has been a long walk—
it flows toward the estuary its future,
the last wide step into a vaster deep,
ancient salt-dark of the churning sea,
great devouring beast to whom
we all at last come (through the long
windings of time): to the wild waters.

VI.

For us who depend upon
these undependable bodies,
a day will arrive that forgets us,
the solitary death we fear—
somehow yanked out of the world,
an image pulled through a picture,
swallowed by the background.

We know the inconceivable
must come,
we see it happen to others,
the closing down of the senses,
and the dimming of the bright islands
of all these days, all terrible nostalgic rages
ruined even as this wide-ranging world,
the wind with its white butterflies,
continues through each death,
oblivious,
                relentless...

Though mourners hold memorials,
in time they are themselves forgotten,
in time their house also becomes the rain,
or the penumbra of the moon, a dark halo...

Those moments when we forget the dead
are dead, as though our memory were
a phantom hand that could touch them,
as if they could speak about the weather
or their long vacation—then!—
relearning their absence is suddenly
weird, more difficult, like fear is difficult—
as if we had taken a wrong turn
into a dream filled with foreign darkness,
or came awake inside a sunken ship
where sea horses coldly dance
on the dining room tables...

Even to ourselves we become
stranger—forgetting who we were,
forgetting somewhere we are still
who we were, when each day was
its own age, and we came to learn
the wide high-wire drone of the cicada,
the killdeer's plaintive panic and dance,
the painted turtle like a solemn
waddling jigsaw puzzle: everything
a beginning to that child for whom
our own lives are the funeral.

And we know the little we manage
to remember will be forgotten,
knowing nations are forgotten,
and the river washes away the ruins
of villages that once drank its water—

I gaze at this hand so familiar
with its lifeline across the tiny
continent of my palm while above
the high winds move the clouds
and I imagine it is a thing uninhabited,
helpless to grasp the simplest tool,
a compass, a ruler, this hand
open to the afternoon sky I imagine
half-eaten by the dimming dusk
floating into the darkening deep.

Leaf,
light,
river,
the sound of the river,
shadow on water—
all are absorbed
into the night:
it is the way things are,
light going away, voice going away,
hands that cannot grasp water
and water shifting its shape,
all drawn toward some end,

the physics of time,
the long stories of evolution,
the stars themselves from which
the myths were hung,
eventually gone, lost...
to entropy—dispersion—
or those great crushing black holes...

It is the way things are: time
flowing out of itself like the river,
its distance a long forgetting,
a fall...
                    as we must fall, and will
without needing to remember how,
forgetting who we are but becoming
the fall...
                            perhaps becoming the glint
of a raindrop falling—
or a voice that seems familiar,
our own echo from the past,
a well whose depth speaks to us—
our voice the voice of falling,
or rivers in autumn that belong
to a distance their own,
or many voices together,
all the grief we've kept
and all of our dead falling with us
toward...
                          what lost waters...

the distance that belongs
to nothing but itself...

VII.

The trees lift and quake in the breeze,
a green shimmering commotion.

And within each translucent leaf
flitting in the glistening light,
atoms quaver with fierce power.

The house of the wind
with its traveling foundation
and turns and gusts,
opens and closes its rooms,
its drafty corridors,
and the whole forest rumors
the shape of its passing.

If I can forget myself and become
a vagabond ghost like the wind
whose house is everywhere,
without number or nation, then
the universe is an enormous dance
that goes on shifting, simultaneously
building and destroying itself
like an architecture of air,

or water or flame, upheavals
of geologies, life, loss, all estates
unfixed...

I study the river, gaze into its layers of water,
its currents catching shadows and light,
shuffling through each other...

—And for a moment I felt invisible waves
surge upon the five roads of my senses,
like the aurora borealis rides
the horizon in its Northern ranges,
its sheer steep electric wings
vaulting over the earth—and:
something leaped past myself
and through all forms and motions,
and deeply within the breeze
and the leaves the breeze moved,
as though I had become the forest,
vast as the forest and far
as the distances of time the river
coursed, become larger than
a body within a womb of air,
become the sky ascending into itself,
and the calm ecstasy everything
really is, all vibration and cataclysm
one absolute shudder infinite,
the dance of Shiva a freed joy,
all parts and particles, light and shadow,

leaf quiver and quake, untouched by terror:
something else, something entirely itself,
everything the intersection of the same
limitless wing...

VIII.

I come to woods where tall poplars
were cut down—their white sturdy boles
that shone luminous under the moon
gave up their strength, each tree
enormous beneath its acres of sky—fell.

Now from those water-seeking turning
roots, thousands of saplings leap,
a dense multitude of thin stalks,
an underground green wave lifting
out of the old year, old energy,
those twisting sinews that anchored
the great foliage in the sky: ancient roots,
connected:
                    one forest—
momentum and moment:
                                        one soil.

IX.

in dark essential correspondence
—Jorge Carrera Andrade

However they came, by whatever long
and strange passage through the dark
biologies, the voices sing—
trill,
        hum,
                warble, serenade, hiss,
cry out,
            voices...
                        a traffic of callings,
through the traveling day, along the roads,
the haunting coo of the mourning dove,
born from the dark of a hollow log,
the jay whose shrill cry like a glass knife
shatters serenity,
                        the crazy crow caw
an alarm seeking a riot, notes in the dusk:
night hawk,
                meadow lark,
                                insect distances...
and in the houses with their liquid windows
where the moonlight swims,
                                voices
behind the doors, speaking to be known
as though being heard—saved.

Voices clear as the cricket cry
inside the vault of evening, they are
calls from beneath the ocean's
collapsing wave—each word
a revolt, hammer or drum building a stair
or another dimension—voices
raised or whispered against the pale hour
of old wood becoming the weather,
nails escaping through rusty holes,
the futility of abandoned buildings
with disorder loosening their seams,
voices that refuse the defeat
of fatal places where silence
enfolds solitude
                                        and ghosts of birds
close their wings to become stones
on the dark side of the moon.

And I know of voices lost—
                                                        people
lost...
          voices that never spoke,
cut down by death squads,
censored by the habit of fear,
voices traveling down alleys,
mumbling to themselves—
                                                    or rolling off
the roofs of bedrooms like dreams of rain,
or flying through the nightmare cities

where clocks put on grotesque faces,
secretive voices falling within themselves,
keeping company with autumn leaves
that swirl around a hollow center
like a ghost hunting its shape,
voices anonymous as a field of wheat,
or chaff, mute labor, worn-out tools,
voices awaiting the hour of speech:

in the lost cities the lost citizens,
their silences shredded by sirens,
a world calling to itself—
                                        tearing itself apart—
poverties, despairs, the inheritances of anger
that cannot surrender—slums where people
live and lose in the laid-low wreckages
landlords call 'rental properties,'
a world demolishing itself from neglect—
voices await the invention of a word—

or:
    from the sharp-shattered ruin of all work
when the slow war becomes sudden,
when power stumbles over its broken mask,
and killing is a way of life, then
in the intervals when the bombings cease,
the subtleties of shadow and quiet
conspire a world that can *hear* a word—
(a world calling to itself)—

remote origins, calling:
the ancient energies:
                                    we are: the need to speak
across the empty spaces between us,
and say:
the houses of the stars are open, the day is wide.

In the far distance I hear children calling
from their world of play. Who can say
where one voice ends, another begins?

X.

I keep returning to earlier times, called
by my home town where I once walked
in light so familiar I felt invisible and whole
—and followed the river gleaming and cool,
its dark waters rippling its mysterious word
through the ways and turns of my seasons.

What have I lost that I keep hunting the past,
called by some earlier dawn, mystified by moon?

And once walking a path like this one
came upon fallen wings, dusty, a hawk
evicted from the shifting rooms of sky.
And thought then how all worries
in time are equalized by the wind,

in time the light hunts all hawks down
darkly in the gloaming where the widening
wings of all shadows enter the night.

And I recall now our twilight play
in the cemetery at the edge of town:
hide and seek among the gravestones
in the stone-eating dusk, the polished monuments
lacquered with a glowing phosphorescence.

The ground became a floating island, all shapes
drifting into the cool spanning dimming world—
our voices riding the old and passing breeze,
far away fell faint into the hills leaning into themselves.

In that slanting, waning light we lay flat
against the earth, hiding on the mounds of graves,
hunting ourselves in the dead city while crickets
told the old gossip of the world acre by acre,
closed the hinges of the sun's rusting minutes.

And all children equal with the dark country
coming on, we hid among those used-up names,
hollow letters engraved in stone as the hunter
stalked us, not knowing how later the hunter
would stalk us, not knowing when we called
alle alle oxen free how later we would learn
some are more free than others, some own power.

In a universe whose law is entropy, where
no power lasts longer than each day that dies,
what do children know who hunt each other
equally? Someone goes unarmed calling
our names, a stranger we once knew
wrapped in moonlight who walks between
all dreams, wearing the face of all children,
the face of all slaves who have scanned
the stars, wearing our own face and calling
alle alle auction free, everybody is also free,
home free, at home the night descends upon
the living and the dead the same.

XI.

I cannot imagine my own annihilation
—Walt Whitman

Huge cottonwood and elm trees
loom over the river—the windy shadows
of their branches are cool dark countries
shifting on the water surface.

I skip a stone across those spaces
into the clear light. It bounces between
sky and water, a wing without will—and sinks.
Nothing rends those shadows—
not a stone, nor a body falling into them.

Only the tree leaning into the river
attracts its black reflection,
growing to meet its disappearance.

Those grains of wood that are its continuity
will weaken and decay—open their spaces...

This elm is the physical memory of itself—
seared into its side is the scar where lightning
walked down its trunk, seeking earthly waters...

But further on I find a hollow stump
where the moon has dined on lost seasons—
the mysteries of night have entered that cavity,
devouring each ring outward, hollow workings...

The river is a long journey that seems longer
the older we are, we're told never the same river,
though always falling the one direction it knows:
down—all griefs learning gravity.

If I let fall the mask the years have fashioned,
this countenance hardened from survival,
if I could find my reflection in these waters,
I would reveal what the decades keep hidden,
the archeologies of my abandoned estates,
remote landscapes and years, my home town
lost to an elusive time zone where

a child-ghost, an invention of moonlight,
haunts the countryside.

It is far away, that town I remember,
city of bridges and rippling waters,
the days purling past each other,
the only place I've ever belonged
where the voice of the meandering river,
the loll of its continuous fall,
still calls me like a vagrant son.

I cannot conceive of any use for a town
invoked by memory-light in a world
that each day learns again to become
a torn edge of a leaf, a mote of dust in the evening,
the maps of empires reduced to cinder or mold.

Will the shadow of myself I must some day
lose altitude to meet bring to ruin
all my ghostly and larger-than-life
lives locked in those distant years,
like a tree crashing, like a continent
breaking apart, my name dismantled?

And yet—*as if imagining were a kind of evidence*,
I *could* imagine a lucid moment, like Narcissus
discovering something dark in his eyes,
a hint of origins, or Rilke among the ancients
who respected grief, the inheritance of my tribe—

I could imagine coming to a place anyone might imagine
in the evening when the dusk gathers its powers
and we feel the moment suspended between
the past and the future as though they are one,
the same thing—and the terrible passions of the earth
for a world always leaving seem to merge
into the light into the dark, as though they are
the same thing—and letting my imagination drift,
as though it were a kind of evidence,
if I could imagine feeling at home in some place
other than my home town, I might imagine
approaching a garden whose flowers float
beyond gravity in the center of absolute midnight,
rooted only in a ghostly air of old pain or caring,
luminescent and pale petals familiar as departures:

where I could gather in my palm
the night dew of dark nostalgias—
waters that would wash my face clean.

XII.

If this river were another time,
if I were walking home
like a child in the night,
what could I remember?

Then the fog would lie in the fields
like the soul of an animal without teeth.

The moon,
enormous on the horizon
in the time of harvest,
would be known,
a white sadness...

Then my dead friends might approach,
dropping from their hands
small pebbles washed smooth from the rivers,
ancient memories they return to the dark earth—
while they like the rivers move on.
In the night their eyes are obsidian—
all the old fires captured.

I do not know how
but my face would be emptied,
like a child's face, sweet, pure—
as though
I were walking a trail I've always known,
like someone in no hurry,
who knows the sun sets on the river,
the moon rises on the river,
the river, sun, and moon
are all the same moment,
all come to the same place.